D1443855

Understanding the Federal Reserve and Monetary Policy

CORONA BREZINA

ROSEN
PUBLISHING®

New York

Published in 2012 by The Rosen Publishing Group, Inc.
29 East 21st Street, New York, NY 10010

Library of Congress Cataloging-in-Publication Data

Brezina, Corona.
Understanding the Federal Reserve and monetary policy / Corona Brezina.—1st ed.
    p. cm.—(Real world economics)
Includes bibliographical references and index.
ISBN 978-1-4488-5567-4 (library binding)
1. Board of Governors of the Federal Reserve System (U.S.).
2. Monetary policy—United States—Juvenile literature.
3. Federal Reserve banks—Juvenile literature.
4. Banks and banking, Central—United States—Juvenile literature. I. Title.
HG2565.B74 2012
332.1'10973—dc22

                                                                2011013332

Manufactured in China

CPSIA Compliance Information: Batch #W12YA: For further information, contact Rosen Publishing, New York, New York, at 1-800-237-9932.

On the cover: The Federal Reserve Building, in Washington, D.C., is the headquarters of the Board of Governors of the Federal Reserve.

Contents

INTRODUCTION

In November of 2010, Federal Reserve chairman Ben Bernanke announced a new measure intended to stimulate the economy. The Federal Reserve—"the Fed"—was planning to purchase $600 billion worth of securities. In effect, this move would inject $600 billion into the banking system, leading to lower interest rates. It would encourage banks to begin lending more freely, while inviting individuals and businesses to make investments and purchases with the newly available low-interest loans and credit. All of this would provide a much-needed spur to economic growth.

Before the Great Recession of 2007–2010, such news would have been unprecedented and shocking. Six hundred billion dollars is a huge sum of money, but Americans had just lived through extraordinary economic times. In 2006, when Bernanke took office as chairman of the Federal Reserve, there were few signs that an economic meltdown was looming. Then the economy quickly deteriorated. The thriving housing market

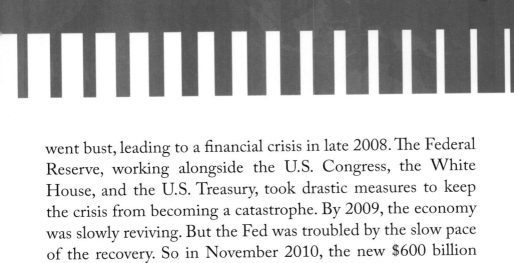

went bust, leading to a financial crisis in late 2008. The Federal Reserve, working alongside the U.S. Congress, the White House, and the U.S. Treasury, took drastic measures to keep the crisis from becoming a catastrophe. By 2009, the economy was slowly reviving. But the Fed was troubled by the slow pace of the recovery. So in November 2010, the new $600 billion program was unveiled.

So what exactly is the Federal Reserve System? The Federal Reserve is the central bank of the United States. A central bank plays a vital role in promoting a nation's economic stability by controlling its money supply. Therefore, during a crisis such as a financial panic, the central bank can take action to stave off potentially disastrous economic consequences. A central bank also regulates all banking operations nationwide and maintains the health of the financial system. In addition, the central bank provides banking services to the government and other institutions.

The Federal Open Market Committee (FOMC) meets in Washington, D.C. The FOMC's monetary policy decisions are a major force in steering the direction of the economy.

With all of these responsibilities, the central bank is a very influential institution. Since the founding of the United States, the precise role of a central bank—and whether one was needed at all—has frequently been a subject of hot debate. Throughout American history, there periodically has been outcry against giving a single entity so much power.

The Federal Reserve was created in 1913. Since then, the duties and functions of the central bank have evolved with the times. New laws and regulations have expanded its scope while also imposing increased accountability to the American people. Fresh controversies over Federal Reserve policies and powers continuously follow in its wake, especially during periods of economic uncertainty or crisis.

CHAPTER ONE

THE ESTABLISHMENT OF THE FEDERAL RESERVE SYSTEM

Soon after the ratification of the Constitution in 1789, the government of the United States began formulating economic policy. President George Washington appointed Alexander Hamilton as secretary of the U.S. Treasury. Hamilton energetically promoted the creation of a central bank. The institution would manage the government's money. It would also serve as a financial regulator and lender of last resort. This means that if a bank was on the brink of failure, the central bank would bail it out.

Granting a government agency this important and powerful role as the nation's financial regulator and controller of the money supply caused considerable controversy. Today, we take it for granted that the federal government controls the money supply and issues currency. Back then, it seemed to many people that having a single entity control the money supply was an unfair means of stifling competition. In addition, there was no standardized form of paper money. Many banks issued their own banknotes. Banknotes issued by the new central bank would be considered legal tender, or official money.

Nonetheless, Hamilton's view that a central bank was essential prevailed, and the First Bank of the United States was created in 1791. Headquartered in Philadelphia, Pennsylvania, it was the nation's largest bank. It was also the biggest corporation of any kind in the entire country. In addition to its role as a central bank, the First Bank also performed some ordinary banking functions. For example, it accepted deposits and made loans to private businesses. For this reason, many state banks regarded the First Bank as a business competitor with an unfair advantage.

Alexander Hamilton, the first secretary of the U.S. Treasury, was the leading advocate for the creation of a central bank that would manage the nation's money and credit.

Ordinary Americans also distrusted the bank. Out of the First Bank's twenty-five directors, five were appointed by the government, and the remaining twenty were selected by private investors. To many people, it seemed that the First Bank of the United States was dominated by wealthy business interests.

In 1811, the First Bank's charter came up for renewal. The First Bank had performed its functions effectively during its twenty-year existence, yet private banks and some political interests opposed renewing the charter. The bill to recharter the bank failed in Congress by one vote.

A Freewheeling Nineteenth Century

After the dissolution of the First Bank, the banking system in the United States quickly became disorganized and ineffective at handling economic crises. Worse, the nation immediately became embroiled in the War of 1812. The government no longer possessed an effective means of managing its money. It even had trouble raising money to finance the war.

By 1816, Congress again supported the concept of a central bank. It approved a charter for the Second Bank of the United States that was even bigger than the First Bank. Yet, like the First Bank, it drew criticism because of the enormous power it held. Nevertheless, the Second Bank never controlled the banking system as effectively as the First Bank. The country had grown in the intervening five years. In the absence of a central bank between 1811 and 1816, each state developed its own banking laws, and the result nationwide was a bewildering and inconsistent patchwork. There were now many more banks to regulate, each operating under a different set of state rules and regulations. Worst of all, many of these banks were on unsound financial footing.

In 1829, Andrew Jackson took office as president. Jackson distrusted banks in general and sought to stir popular resentment against the powerful Second Bank. Congress voted to recharter the Second Bank in 1832, but Jackson vetoed the bill. He went on to take government deposits out of the Second Bank and otherwise impede its functioning. The Second Bank shut down in 1836.

A year later, a financial panic led to a wave of bank failures, and the country slid into a deep economic depression. This began a chaotic period sometimes called the "free banking era." People could open "free banks" without even obtaining a bank charter. Banks all issued their own banknotes. There was no federal regulation of the banking system and no single currency that had reliable, government-backed value.

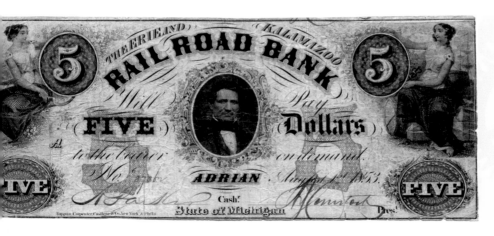

In 1837, Michigan began the "free banking era" when it became the first state to allow individuals to open banks without a charter. Banks could issue their own banknotes, which varied in value.

The Civil War broke out in 1861. The nation was already struggling with yet another economic depression, and now the Union government needed a functional national banking system in place to manage the costs of the war. The National Banking Act of 1863 created a system of nationally chartered banks authorized to issue official U.S. currency. The act also imposed a 10 percent tax on state banknotes, thereby discouraging the issuing and use of state currency. This effectively led to the establishment of a national currency.

Still, there was no centralized banking authority at this time. The nation's economy grew rapidly after the Civil War ended, but it was also a period of volatile "boom or bust" cycles. A financial panic could trigger bank runs, where depositors rushed to banks to take out money that they feared would otherwise be lost to them. If the bank could not meet the sudden demand for withdrawals, it could go bust and the depositors would lose their money. A severe financial panic, such as the Panic of 1893, could trigger a larger and longer-lasting economic depression.

THE FEDERAL RESERVE ACT

Yet another financial crisis—the Panic of 1907—served as a wake-up call to politicians and bankers alike. It was not possible for the modern U.S. economy to remain stable without the guidance of a central bank. In 1908, Congress passed the Aldrich-Vineland Act, which authorized issuance of emergency currency during financial crises. It also set up the National Monetary Commission, headed by Senator Nelson Aldrich, to recommend a series of reforms to the financial system.

In 1911, the commission released its plan. It called for a National Reserve Association with branches in cities across the country. The National Reserve would issue currency and oversee member banks. Most of the members of the board of directors would be selected by banks, not by the government.

The plan drew heated opposition. To many, it seemed that the National Monetary Commission's proposals gave too much control to big business and the banking industry. In addition, the political climate was shifting in Washington. Aldrich was a Republican, yet elections in 1910 and 1912 gave Democrats control of Congress and the White House. Woodrow Wilson, the new president, had railed against the concentration of power in a central bank during his campaign. Ultimately, the Aldrich plan was rejected, but Wilson was wise enough to recognize the limits of his economic expertise. He charged representatives Carter Glass and H. Parker Willis with developing a plan alternate to that put forth by Aldrich and the National Monetary Commission.

Glass and Willis proposed the creation of a network of regional reserve banks. Wilson tweaked the plan, adding a central board that would coordinate efforts among the regional branches. Members would be appointed by the president, not by banks as in the Aldrich plan.

The Federal Reserve Act was formally introduced in Congress in 1913, setting off months of political debate. Some politicians considered the bill too favorable to bankers, while bankers objected to the increased government oversight of the financial industry. Wilson personally met with skeptical members of Congress to bolster support for the act. Finally, in late December, the Federal Reserve Act was passed and signed into law.

President Woodrow Wilson signs the Federal Reserve Act into law on December 23, 1913. The act was a compromise that drew the support of diverse political and business interests.

President Wilson nominated five members to the Federal Reserve Board and, after sharp and bitter debate, the Senate confirmed the nominations. The Federal Reserve officially opened its doors on November 16, 1914.

AN EVOLVING INSTITUTION

In negotiating the details of the Federal Reserve Act, Wilson emphasized to members of Congress that the details of the bill could be subject to amendment at a later time. This has proved true over the course of the Fed's century-long existence.

The Panic of 1907

The Panic of 1907 began when a group of speculators failed to corner the copper market. In the aftermath, the public learned that financial trust companies in New York had made bad loans to these speculators. This news triggered a nationwide bank run. The third largest of the trust companies, the Knickerbocker Trust Company, collapsed after its customers withdrew $8 million in three hours on October 21. Soon, several smaller trusts failed. The panic spread to the stock market, and stocks dropped sharply.

New York banker and financier J. P. Morgan stepped in to avert a complete, nationwide economic meltdown. He convinced other bank presidents to help bail out the stock market and make loans to keep struggling banks afloat. At one point, Morgan locked fifty trust presidents in his library until they worked out an agreement on a $25 million loan to keep New York City out of bankruptcy.

Though the immediate panic ended by the first week of 1908, it triggered a recession. The economy did not fully recover until 1910. The incident highlighted the need for financial reform. J. P. Morgan had staved off disaster, but it had become clear that the nation needed a central bank to regulate its banks and set monetary policy, thereby creating economic stability. There was no guarantee that in the future someone like Morgan would be able to orchestrate an emergency rescue plan. With a central bank overseeing the banking system, the likelihood of economic chaos and the need for such drastic emergency measures would be greatly reduced.

Most of the legislation affecting the Federal Reserve was passed in response to financial crises or new developments in the banking and financial sector. For example, Congress passed several major reforms in the aftermath of the Great Depression.

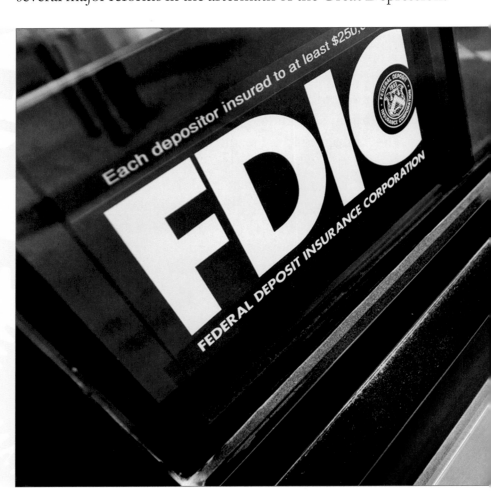

A failed bank displays a Federal Deposit Insurance Corporation (FDIC) decal. Because of the FDIC, customers do not lose all of their money—they are generally guaranteed up to $250,000—when a financial institution fails.

The Banking Act of 1933—also known as the Glass-Steagall Act—placed new limitations on banks and increased Federal Reserve oversight. It also established the Federal Deposit Insurance Corporation (FDIC). This meant that if a bank

failed, depositors would no longer lose all of their money but would be compensated by the federal government for at least some of it. The Banking Act of 1935 modified the structure of the Federal Reserve, creating a Board of Governors in addition to other changes.

After the end of World War II, the Employment Act of 1946 directed that the Federal Reserve should promote maximum employment as one of its missions. In 1951, the Treasury-Federal Reserve Accord drew a dividing line between the powers of the U.S. Treasury and those of the Federal Reserve. The accord essentially granted the Federal Reserve independence from influence of the other branches of government. This gave the Federal Reserve more flexibility—and more power—in determining monetary policy.

In 1980, the Depository Institutions Deregulation and Monetary Control Act set off a period of major reforms in banking laws. Many Fed officials believed that strict banking regulations were putting banks at a disadvantage compared to other financial institutions. Banks could now, for example, offer interest-bearing checking accounts, which had previously been prohibited. As the trend toward deregulation continued, another notable piece of legislation was enacted: the 1999 Gramm-Leach-Bliley Act. This essentially reversed the Glass-Steagall Act of 1933. It permitted banks to offer an expanded range of financial services, such as insurance and investment banking.

The 1990s was a decade of economic expansion. After 9/11, effective guidance from the Federal Reserve was credited with minimizing the economic impact of the terrorist attacks. To many, the Federal Reserve seemed infallible. But this illusion of infallibility was shattered in 2008, when a financial crisis sent the country spinning into a severe and long-lasting recession.

CHAPTER TWO

WHAT DOES THE FEDERAL RESERVE DO?

As the central bank of the United States, the Federal Reserve performs a crucial role in guiding the nation's economy. The chairman of the Federal Reserve Board is a very important public official. When the chairman makes a statement, the bankers on Wall Street pay close attention. So do members of the general public. Decisions made by the Federal Reserve impact banks' profitability. They also affect the investments and mortgages of ordinary people.

THE FED'S MAIN RESPONSIBILITIES

Most people appreciate that the Federal Reserve is a powerful institution, but the Fed's duties are even broader than generally recognized. The Federal Reserve fulfills four basic functions.

The Federal Reserve conducts the nation's monetary policy. This means that the Fed controls the money supply by influencing the flow of money and credit in the economy. Ultimately, this affects the overall level of spending in the economy.

The nation's money supply includes currency, which is paper money and coins, as well as checkable deposits, which is money that can be drawn from a checking account.

The Federal Reserve also has the authority to supervise and regulate banking operations. The Fed ensures that banks are complying with relevant laws, for example, and approves bank mergers. It works with the FDIC to provide a safety net in case of bank failure. The Fed also sets rules and enforces laws that provide protection to ordinary people in financial matters.

Another function of the Federal Reserve is to provide services to depository institutions. This includes financial institutions such as mutual savings banks, savings and loan associations, and credit unions, as well as commercial banks. Federal Reserve Banks distribute cash and coins to depository institutions so that customers can make withdrawals. The Federal Reserve clears checks. Whenever a check is taken to a bank, the Fed ultimately transfers the payment by crediting one bank's Federal Reserve account and debiting another. The Federal Reserve also manages wire transfers and automated clearinghouses. These are electronic means of transferring money and making payments.

In addition, the Federal Reserve acts as banker to the U.S. government. It maintains the nation's payment system, which conducts financial transactions between government agencies and other institutions. The U.S. Treasury and other government agencies make deposits and withdrawals in their Federal Reserve accounts. The government draws on these accounts for Social Security payments, the payroll for federal employees, and much more. Some types of tax payments are deposited into these accounts as well.

THE STRUCTURE OF THE FEDERAL RESERVE

The Federal Reserve is overseen by the seven-member Board of Governors, which is headquartered in Washington, D.C. The

21

governors are nominated by the president and must be confirmed by the Senate. Each governor serves a fourteen-year term. A nomination for governor comes up every two years. A chairman and vice chairman of the Fed are nominated by the president from among the Board of Governors membership. They serve four-year terms.

The Board of Governors meets regularly with members of three advisory councils: the Consumer Advisory Council, the Community Depository Institutions Advisory Council, and the Federal Advisory Council. These councils keep the board informed of the needs and concerns of different sectors of the financial industry. In addition, board members commonly consult with government officials and financial executives.

The Federal Reserve Board is charged with implementing the nation's monetary policy. It regulates and supervises banks and other financial institutions. It has authority over the nation's payment system. It also administers consumer protection regulations.

The Federal Reserve is sometimes referred to as a "decentralized central bank." This is because of the relative autonomy of its twelve district Reserve Banks. The regional headquarters are based in Boston, Massachusetts; New York City; Philadelphia, Pennsylvania; Cleveland, Ohio; Richmond, Virginia; Atlanta, Georgia; Chicago, Illinois; St. Louis, Missouri; Minneapolis, Minnesota; Kansas City, Missouri; Dallas, Texas; and San Francisco, California. There are also branches in twenty-five other cities across the United States. The district boundaries reflect the population distribution in the country when the Fed began operations in 1914. For this reason, the entire West Coast is served by only one Federal Reserve Bank—the San Francisco Federal Reserve.

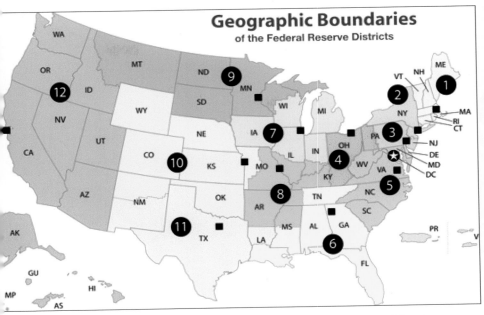

Geographic Boundaries
of the Federal Reserve Districts

After the passage of the Federal Reserve Act, cities vied for the privilege—and resulting clout—of being chosen as the site of a Reserve Bank. The banks and their districts are shown above.

Every Federal Reserve Bank has a nine-member board of directors that appoints a president. Three of the directors represent the banking industry. The other six represent the general public and economic interests outside the banking industry. Each Federal Reserve Bank is independently incorporated, although it does not operate for a profit. If the bank does make a profit over the course of the year, these funds are returned to the U.S. Treasury.

The Reserve Banks operate as "banker's banks"—they provide financial services to the banks and other depository institutions in their districts. They also supervise and regulate banks and act as the banker for U.S. government agencies. In addition, Reserve Banks conduct important research into key economic issues, helping to direct national policy.

The Federal Reserve's monetary policy is formulated by a twelve-member group called the Federal Open Market Committee (FOMC). The seven-member Board of Governors and the president of the New York Federal Reserve Bank serve on the FOMC. The other four members are presidents of district Reserve Banks, who serve on a rotating basis. All of the district Reserve Bank presidents attend FOMC meetings and participate in policy discussion. The FOMC is charged with directing open market operations, one of the Fed's crucial monetary policy tools (which will be discussed shortly).

Commercial banks can opt to become members of the Federal Reserve System. There are certain requirements, such as subscribing to stock in the District Reserve Bank. All nationally chartered banks

The interest rates targeted by the Federal Reserve impact how much interest consumers pay on their mortgages, as well as on other types of loans.

are required to belong to the Federal Reserve System. State-chartered banks can choose to join the Reserve. Other types of depository institutions are subject to Federal Reserve regulations and have access to some Fed services and protections.

Monetary Policy Tools

The Fed steers monetary policy primarily by influencing the nation's money supply. When the Fed changes the interest rate—which affects the money supply—it's major news in the business world. Lower interest rates encourage borrowing from banks and use of credit to make purchases. More money circulates throughout the economy. Higher interest rates discourage borrowing and use of credit, and less cash circulates throughout the economy. Because interest rates affect the availability and cost of credit, they are a matter of great importance to financial institutions and individual borrowers alike. Credit is money available for borrowing. It gives a person or institution an opportunity to make purchases and pay for them later. The lender benefits by charging interest on the loan.

The Federal Reserve uses three main tools in directing monetary policy. The first is open market operations. Open market operations, the most flexible and commonly used tool, are directed by the FOMC. This is the buying and selling of government securities on the open market. Government securities are bonds and other debt obligations issued by the U.S. Treasury that are bought and sold as investments. Open market operations are conducted at the Open Market Desk at the New York Federal Reserve.

Fiscal Policy and the Economy

The Federal Reserve uses monetary policy to achieve its objectives. However, the U.S. government employs a different tool kit to influence the economy: fiscal policy. Fiscal policy is the use of government spending and taxation to bring about desired economic goals. Since it involves the nation's budget, fiscal policy is controlled by the president and Congress. During a recession, both monetary policy and fiscal policy are employed to bring about a turnaround. Congress and the president will likely increase government spending and cut taxes in order to stimulate economic growth. This often results in a budget deficit, in which government spending exceeds revenue from taxes. Once the economy is in recovery, the government must address the matter of deficits, perhaps by cutting spending or raising taxes.

The FOMC sets monetary policy by issuing a target federal funds rate. The federal funds rate is the interest rate that one bank charges another when making unsecured loans of reserve balances at Federal Reserve Banks overnight. How is this affected by open market operations? Depending on the target federal funds rate, the Fed will either buy or sell securities. If the Fed wants the target rate to move down, it buys securities, increasing the amount of reserves in the banking system. The banks now have more money to lend and invest, and cash flows into the economy. This will cause the actual federal funds rate to fall in line with the Fed's target. Conversely, if the Fed wants the target rate to increase, it will sell off securities. Banks' reserves decline, and, as a result, they curtail investing and lending, and money exits the economy.

Another monetary tool employed by the Fed is the discount rate. It is set by the boards of directors of the Reserve Banks. The discount rate is the interest rate that the Fed charges depository institutions for short-term loans made at a department referred to as the "discount window" of a Reserve Bank. The discount rate is changed relatively seldom.

The Fed's third monetary policy tool is the reserve requirement. Banks must set aside a percentage of their deposit—about 10 percent—as reserves, either as cash in the bank vault or deposited in their Reserve Bank. If the Fed were to raise the reserve requirement, the banks would have to set aside more of their funds, decreasing the amount of money available to lend and draining cash from the economy. The reserve requirement is the Fed's least-used tool. A change in the reserve requirement indicates a major shift in monetary policy.

Behind the Scenes

Eight times a year, the FOMC convenes for a meeting where members discuss the state of the economy and determine the target federal funds rate. The policy decisions that result from these meetings are closely watched in the financial industry. Sometimes the Fed's announcements are widely reported in the national media as well, especially during uncertain economic times or when the Fed shifts course.

Members of the Federal Open Market Committee hear reports on current economic conditions and future trends during one of the FOMC's regular meetings.

Two weeks before an FOMC meeting, a report called the Beige Book is released. The Beige Book summarizes economic conditions in the twelve districts. FOMC members will also have conferred with financial experts and received a briefing from their research departments.

FOMC meetings generally last one or two days. Nineteen participants (twelve FOMC members and seven Federal Reserve Bank presidents) attend, as well as staff members and economists. The meeting begins with reports of economic statistics and trends. Next is a "go-round," in which Board members and Reserve presidents discuss district and national economic conditions. This discussion period helps ensure that Fed recommendations will consider both national and regional concerns. FOMC members then hear an outline of possible policy options: an increase, a decrease, or no change in the target federal funds rate. In a second go-round, they make their cases for various options. The chairman then makes a policy proposal based on these discussions.

At the end of the meeting, the twelve FOMC members cast a vote on the proposal. Shortly afterward, the FOMC announces its policy decision along with an explanation. The new targeted federal funds rate will be implemented through transactions on the Open Market Trading Desk.

Ten Great Questions
to Ask an Economics Teacher

1 What is the current federal funds rate?

2 What is the current rate of inflation?

3 What did the latest FOMC statement indicate about the state of the economy?

4 How is the Fed taking action to keep down rates of inflation and unemployment?

5 Are there any current international trends that could impact the U.S. economy?

6 Have the Fed chairman or other Fed officials raised any specific economic concerns lately in speeches or congressional testimony?

7 What Federal Reserve district do I live in, and who is the president of my Federal Reserve Bank?

8 Are there any pressing economic concerns specific to my region?

9 How does the Fed guarantee the soundness of my bank and other financial institutions?

10 How does the Fed protect consumers in their financial transactions?

CHAPTER THREE
THE FED IN ACTION

The original Federal Reserve Act and subsequent laws clearly define the Fed's mission.

The Federal Reserve's monetary policy tools make it a very powerful institution. It is, however, subject to congressional legislation.

The Federal Reserve is charged with using monetary policy to fulfill three specific objectives. It is charged with maintaining price stability, supporting stable long-term interest rates, and sustaining maximum employment among the workforce. More generally, the Fed is expected to foster sustainable economic growth and support sound financial markets.

The Fed can achieve its first objective—stable prices—by influencing the money supply. If the money supply increases, there is more money available to buy the same number of goods. As a result, prices increase. The Fed's goals of maintaining stable prices and interest rates, however, sometimes conflict with its mission of maximizing employment. Low interest rates tend to stimulate the economy, resulting in increased lending, spending, and employment. But low interest rates also increase the money supply, causing prices to rise. In the long term, this policy could damage the economy. The Fed must balance the two goals—price stability and high employment—depending on economic circumstances at any particular time. This task can prove especially difficult during periods of economic uncertainty.

MONETARY POLICY AND THE BUSINESS CYCLE

The economy tends to fluctuate through periods of growth alternating with occasional downturns. This phenomenon is called the business cycle. It consists of four phases: peak, recession, trough, and expansion. The peak is the highest point in economic growth. A recession is a decline in growth. After the downturn, the cycle reaches the trough, the lowest point in economic growth. It is followed by a recovery and resultant economic expansion.

The Federal Reserve makes its monetary policy decisions depending on where the economy lies within the business cycle. During a recession, the Fed generally pursues expansionary monetary policy. That is, it tries to increase the money supply and get cash circulating through the economy again. To achieve this, the Fed lowers interest rates, which increases the money supply and encourages economic growth. During periods of economic expansion, the Fed's main concern is maintaining sustainable economic growth. It may raise interest rates to slow the short-term rate of expansion, avoid flooding the economy with cash, and keep inflation and prices at moderate levels. This will support long-term economic stability.

The Fed's actions are major news events during an economic downturn. Here, the Dow Jones ticker in New York's Times Square displays the latest update during the Great Recession.

Since 1950, the U.S. economy has experienced ten recessions lasting between eight and eighteen months. In between these periods of recession, however, were long stretches of steady economic growth. This is a testament to the general effectiveness of Fed policies in both combating recession and

promoting a return to and maintenance of economic expansion and stability.

During these years, the Federal Reserve's primary goal has been maintaining price stability. In particular, the Federal Reserve has worked to fight inflation. Inflation is an economic trend in which price levels of goods and services increase. Today, a dollar does not go as far as it did in the past. Say that you spend $50 on various goods and services today. In 1970, the same amount of goods and services would have cost less than $10. This is the result of inflation. On average, each year brings a slight increase in prices. When prices increase, the value of the dollar—what it can buy—decreases. And very often, salaries and wages do not keep up with the inflation rate, so the purchasing power of individuals and families can decrease over time.

When inflation levels are high, business leaders and ordinary consumers grow uncertain about how to plan for the future. Workers worry about whether their wages will keep up with the rate of inflation. Inflation affects peoples' savings—a fixed amount of money in a savings account will quickly lose value during a period of high inflation. This discourages saving money and hurts people who have to live off their savings or a fixed income, like Social Security or pension payments. Bankers are often forced to charge higher interest rates on loans to compensate for the gradual loss in value of loan repayments during periods of high inflation.

Consumer spending declined during the Great Recession, impacting business profits. Shoppers often find great bargains by taking advantage of clearance sales at stores forced to close their doors.

During a recession, the inflation rate tends to fall. In fact, recessions bring the danger of deflation, the opposite of inflation. Deflation is a general decrease in price levels of goods and services. Although lower prices might sound like a good deal for shoppers, it leads to lower profits for businesses and has an overall negative effect on the economy. If businesses make lower profits, they lay off workers. Unemployed workers do not have the money to buy the things they used to, so goods go unsold and prices fall further. Profits continue to decrease, and more layoffs ensue. A deflationary spiral has begun. Happily, the United States has not experienced an episode of severe deflation since the Great Depression.

Alan Greenspan (1926–)

Appointed chairman of the Federal Reserve Board by President Ronald Reagan in 1987, Alan Greenspan served in the post under four different U.S. presidents. He presided, for the most part, over an era of stable economic expansion. Unemployment levels and the inflation rate remained low. The economy experienced just two mild recessions. Greenspan impressed Democratic and Republican lawmakers alike with his management of crises, as well as his day-to-day handling of the Fed. When he stepped down in 2006, his performance on the job was almost universally praised.

Since then, Greenspan's reputation has waned. Many economists blame Fed policy, in part, for the housing bubble that led to the financial crisis. They point to insufficient regulation of the financial sector, along with the low federal funds rate between 2002 and 2005. Greenspan has maintained that it wasn't the Fed's job to prevent asset bubbles.

MONETARY POLICY THROUGH THE YEARS

Early on, the Fed had less autonomy than it does today. It largely supported the Treasury's economic policies. In the early 1920s, the Fed sought to expand its ability to determine and affect monetary policy. As a result, it established open market operations as a new policy tool. An expanded tool kit would prove essential as the late 1920s ushered in a period of economic chaos.

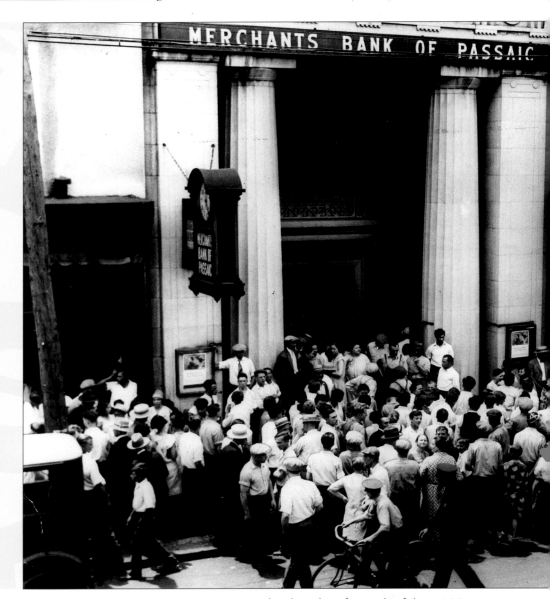

Customers swarm a New Jersey bank in the aftermath of the 1929 stock market crash. Today, bank runs are a thing of the past due to reform measures enacted after the Great Depression.

During the Roaring Twenties, ordinary people, seeking to reap the benefits of postwar affluence and partake of some of the many new consumer goods suddenly available (such as cars, radios, and kitchen appliances), increasingly spent on credit and went into debt. All of this consumer spending, along with frenzied investment in stocks, made the stock market surge. Yet many of these investments were highly speculative (not based on a company's history of sound performance but upon wildly inflated and unfounded hopes for future profits) and thus were risky.

In 1928, the Federal Reserve attempted to rein in this risky speculation in the stock market by raising interest rates. It hoped that by raising the rates, cash would exit the economy, and all the spending and investing would cool before a personal debt crisis and burst stock market bubble would devastate the economy. Yet despite the Fed's efforts, the economy moved into a recession by mid-1929. The stock market crashed in late 1929, marking the beginning of the worst economic contraction in U.S. history. Many economists believe that the Fed's actions were partially responsible for both the economic slowdown and the stock market crash.

Between 1929 and 1933, the gross domestic product (GDP)—the value of all goods and services produced in the U.S. economy—fell by about 30 percent. Levels of unemployment reached 25 percent. A high rate of deflation further choked the possibility of recovery. Many borrowers defaulted on their loans or declared bankruptcy.

The Great Depression brought disaster to the banking system. Over 20 percent of the nation's banks failed, and many others merged with other banks. The reduction in the number of banks decreased the nation's money supply, further contributing to general economic hardship. Surviving banks were wary about issuing new loans during such dire economic times, fearing that people wouldn't be able to repay them. Though the banking system was extremely fragile at this time, the Federal Reserve made no move to aid it. The Fed leadership believed that only weak banks would fail, and the stronger banks could pick up the slack and fill any void created by bank failures. Nor did the Fed move to drastically cut interest rates to stimulate growth.

In 1932, under pressure from Congress, the Fed finally did take action to increase the money supply. The economy began to stabilize. But the Fed reversed this policy later in the year, and the economy began to decline once again.

When President Franklin D. Roosevelt took office in 1933, he immediately took steps to address the banking crisis. He wished to bypass the Fed, which had proved to be ineffective and reluctant to act during much of the economic crisis. Roosevelt ordered banks to be shut down during a bank "holiday." They were only allowed to reopen after they had proved their financial soundness. New regulations further stabilized the system and restored confidence in banks. Roosevelt also removed the dollar from the gold standard. Before, the value of the dollar was tied to the price of gold. Abandoning the gold standard gave the Fed greater control over monetary policy. The economy began to grow slowly after 1933, although it took time to reach prosperity once again.

The next major challenge for the Federal Reserve resulted from a period of drastic inflation during the 1970s and early 1980s. One root cause was a sharp increase in the price of oil between 1973 and 1974, which drove up prices for many other commodities, products, and consumer goods. Economists coined a new term, "stagflation," to describe the combined effect of high inflation, stagnant economic growth, and a high unemployment rate.

The Federal Reserve was slow to take action. Until this point, fighting inflation had not been one of the Fed's primary objectives. In addition, infighting among policy makers delayed any decisive steps. By 1979, with inflation reaching an extremely high level of 13.3 percent, economists agreed that it had to be reined in. Late in the year, the Fed announced that it was moving to tighten the money supply—mainly by raising interest rates—and let the market determine the federal funds rate. This action caused short-term economic hardship. The economy dipped into a recession, interest rates soared, and the unemployment rate increased. In the long term, though, it brought the rate of inflation down to sustainable levels. This, in turn, promoted consumer confidence and spending and increased corporate profits, industrial production, and hiring.

In 1987, Alan Greenspan was appointed chairman of the Board of Governors of the Federal Reserve. Two months later, the stock market experienced its worst crash in history. On October 19, it lost 22.6 percent of its value. In response, the

Bankers stand outside the New York Stock Exchange following the "Black Monday" stock market crash of 1987, which impacted markets around the world.

Federal Reserve used open market operations to lower the federal funds rate, pumping money into the banking system. The Fed also urged the New York Stock Exchange to remain open and operate as usual, rather than shut its doors and halt trading. This measure was taken in order to prevent the further erosion of stock value and loss of money. Greenspan publicly pledged to support the soundness of the economic and financial system. The Fed's capable response was credited with minimizing the consequences of the crash and laying the groundwork for the stock market's—and the larger economy's—relatively quick recovery.

Greenspan steered the economy through a very prosperous decade during the 1990s. In 2001, the world—and the financial system—was shocked by the 9/11 terrorist attacks. The disaster could have caused an economic crisis. To prevent this, the Federal Reserve reacted immediately by lowering the federal funds rate and assuring banks that their "liquidity needs" would be met. This meant that the Fed would keep money flowing so that banks could continue making payments. The Fed's actions helped the economy recover quickly from the immediate after-effects of the attacks.

Greenspan's term as chairman was such a success that he was considered a superstar, both in economic circles and beyond. But late in his tenure, doubts began to arise in some quarters about the long-term consequences of his policies.

MYTHS and FACTS

ABOUT THE FEDERAL RESERVE

MYTH The Federal Reserve is controlled by political interests in the government.

FACT The Fed is a government agency that operates with considerable independence. It derives its mandate from the Federal Reserve Act and is subject to congressional legislation. The president appoints the board members, and they must be approved by Congress. After that, the president and Congress do not control the Fed's decisions and actions.

MYTH Federal Reserve Banks are not adequately held accountable in their financial dealings.

FACT The Federal Reserve System, the Board of Governors, and each Reserve Bank are all regularly audited. The results are made public in annual reports. The Government Accountability Office (GAO) also has the authority to investigate some Fed activities. In addition, the board has an Office of Inspector General, and each Reserve Bank has an internal auditor.

MYTH The Federal Reserve is more interested in looking out for big banks than the welfare of the American people.

FACT After the financial crisis of 2007–2010, there was outcry over the government and the Fed bailing out big financial institutions. Many people believed that since the banks had brought about their dire situation through risky investments, they didn't deserve to be rescued. The truth, however, is that a collapse of the financial system would have devastated the American economy. Whether or not the banks "deserved" to be saved, it was viewed by the Fed, many economists, and outside observers as a necessary action.

CHAPTER FOUR

THE FED AND THE GREAT RECESSION

During the first few years of the twenty-first century, many Americans—even lower-income Americans—achieved the dream of owning their own home. In the excitement of the housing boom, banks issued loans to many subprime borrowers—people who often lacked the means to repay their loans. The value of these homes quickly increased. When the housing bubble collapsed, however, prices of homes dropped and borrowers began defaulting on their loans. This created huge losses for the financial institutions that had made investments based on home mortgages.

As the crisis unfolded, many economists and ordinary Americans were left wondering how this could have happened. How did the housing bubble grow out of control? Why wasn't any regulatory agency monitoring the financial soundness of the big banks and financial institutions and the wisdom of their loans and loan policies? How did the downfall of one economic sector—housing—cause such widespread devastation to the overall economy?

ROOTS OF THE GREAT RECESSION

Much of the blame for the Great Recession of 2007–2010 fell on the banking industry. Banks had made bad loans and engaged in risky investment practices. But the Federal Reserve also received harsh criticism.

When the economy faltered in 2001 following the 9/11 terrorist attacks, the Fed cut interest rates to counteract the downturn. The federal funds rate dropped to 1 percent—the lowest rate in forty-five years. In 2004, the rate began inching upward again, but very slowly. These extraordinarily low interest rates made credit easily available to borrowers, many of whom were not well-positioned to repay it. Because of the low interest rates, investors began taking financial risks in order to make a greater profit.

The Federal Reserve failed to rein in reckless behavior in the financial industry. It did not attempt to restrain subprime lending, even though many economists were worried that banks were urging borrowers to take out loans that they would not be able to repay. Nor did the Fed attempt to expand regulation of new financial products. For example, investment banks could buy a pool of mortgages and slice them up. These pieces were rebundled with pieces of other loans of varying levels of risks. The resulting investment packages were sold to investors around the world. As a result, a broad range of different investments were dependent on risky subprime mortgages, though this wasn't always clear to the investors who bought them.

When the housing bubble burst, the damage affected the entire banking system. Amid plummeting housing values and

Rates of home foreclosures reached record levels during the Great Recession. In addition to devastating individual homeowners, foreclosures can drag down property values throughout a neighborhood.

BANK FORECLOSURE SALE

(6) 3 BEDROOM, 3.5 BATH LUXURY TOWNHOMES

- ELEGANT & SPACIOUS
- CLOSED CIRCUIT CAMERA SECURITY
- QUALITY LAMINATE & CARPET FLOORS
- KITCHENS W/CUSTOM CABINETS
- STAINLESS STEEL APPLIANCES

- RECESSED LIGHTING
- WASHER & DRYER HOO
- 2 CAR PARKING
- LARGE MASTER SUITE 2/SUN D
- PARTIAL VIEW FROM TOP FLOO

OPEN HOUSE SAT-SUN 1-5
EXCEPT HOLIDAYS

자세한 문의에게
제인 문 에게

로 전화하십

REAL ESTATE PEOPLE

rising loan and mortgage defaults, nobody knew the exact value of the mortgage-based investments. Banks grew nervous about lending out money in this climate, leading to a credit crunch and a cash-starved economy. As a result, consumer and business spending plummeted, profits fell, layoffs ensued, and the economy tipped into a deep recession.

The Great Recession: By the Numbers

Beginning in 2008, a financial crisis triggered the worst economic crisis in the United States since the Great Depression. A housing bubble burst, leading to a credit crisis that shook the global economy. Banks and financial institutions collapsed or survived only due to government bailouts. The stock market's Dow Jones Industrial Average is a stock index that measures the trading performance of thirty large American corporations. It is considered a good benchmark, or gauge of the stock market's economic health. It had reached a high of 14,164 in October of 2007, but closed at 6,547 in March of 2009, before beginning to inch upward again.

The economy lost hundreds of thousands of jobs every month during late 2008 and 2009. The unemployment rate soared, reaching a high of 10.2 percent in late 2009. People saw the value of their investments and retirement plans plummet. Rates of home foreclosures increased dramatically as borrowers found themselves unable to meet their mortgage payments. The economy contracted sharply—during the first quarter of 2009, the GDP declined 6.4 percent. The federal budget deficit ballooned due to increased government spending and lower revenue, leading to a national debt level of more than $14 trillion.

Dealing with the Crisis

During an economic downturn, the Fed lowers the federal funds rate, increasing the money supply and promoting the infusion of cash into a parched economy. By the end of 2008, the federal funds rate stood close to 0.0 percent, the lowest possible value.

The depth of the economic crisis put the Federal Reserve in new economic territory. How could the Fed continue to implement monetary policy when its primary monetary tool had reached its absolute limit? The federal funds rate could be cut no further. The Fed was forced to turn to "nontraditional policy tools." Essentially, this means going on a federal spending spree and pumping money into banks so that they can continue to make loans and honor deposits. Economists called it "credit easing." This new set of policy tools achieved two goals. It increased the availability of money and credit. It also helped bail out certain troubled financial institutions that were considered too big to fail. If these institutions collapsed, the Fed argued, the consequences on the overall economy would be far greater than the cost of rescuing them.

Initially, Federal Reserve Chairman Ben Bernanke was reluctant to take drastic intervention. The first victim of the economic crisis was Bear Stearns, a financial institution that was not subject to Fed regulation or protection. In March of 2008, however, the Federal Reserve departed from its usual role and loaned Bear Stearns billions of dollars to keep it from failing. But at this point, the Fed became wary of bailing out every ailing financial institution. In September, the Fed and Treasury did not act to prevent the giant investment bank Lehman Brothers from collapsing. Later, many analysts would judge this a huge mistake.

Many ordinary Americans hurt by the recession were infuriated by government bailouts of big financial corporations, which they viewed as condoning and rewarding risky investment practices.

The collapse of Lehman Brothers sent the financial system spinning into chaos. At this point, Bernanke realized that extreme measures were indeed necessary to rescue the economy. Two days later, the Fed bailed out the insurance giant AIG with a loan of $85 billion. The Fed also focused on relieving

the credit crunch. It set up new procedures for financial institutions to obtain short-term credit. In addition to lending, the Fed devised new means of guaranteeing liquidity—making money for transactions easily available to borrowers and investors. These new programs meant that in order to inject money into the economy, the Fed was buying up certain types of assets from troubled financial institutions, even though it had never dealt with these kinds of assets before. The Fed recognized the need to support the mortgage and housing market. In early 2009, the Fed began a program of buying up mortgage-backed securities. It authorized $1.25 trillion worth of purchases throughout the year.

CHAPTER FIVE

MONETARY POLICY IN A MODERN GLOBAL ECONOMY

The Great Recession was a global economic downturn. In the autumn of 2008, even as Bernanke and other Federal Reserve officials were dealing with the financial crisis in the United States, they were also communicating with their counterparts in other nations. The toxic mortgage-backed securities that had caused the collapse of the U.S. housing market, the crisis among financial institutions, and the freezing of credit had also been traded on international financial markets.

For this reason, nations across the world were also seeing stock market volatility, failing financial institutions, and a frozen credit market. In some instances, the Federal Reserve coordinated its relief measures with other nations' central banks in order to stabilize the international financial system. Across the globe, central banks cut interest rates and flooded the financial system with money. As the financial crisis led to a recession, many governments enacted stimulus plans to bolster an economic recovery.

The crisis underscored the degree to which the economies of the world are now interconnected. Today, uncertainty in one nation's economy can lead to global repercussions and instability.

INTERNATIONAL MONETARY POLICY

The Federal Reserve formulates monetary policy based on the needs of the U.S. economy. International economic policy is primarily decided by the U.S. Treasury. Nonetheless, the

The New York Federal Reserve Bank, which offers tours of its massive gold vault, is the largest and most powerful branch of the Federal Reserve.

FOMC considers international trends and developments when debating monetary policy. Changes in exchange rates of the dollar with other currencies, for example, can impact the U.S. economy. Fed officials also maintain communication with other central banks on issues of common concern. In addition, it regulates foreign banks operating within the United States.

The Fed works closely with the Treasury in international economic affairs. It is possible for the Fed and the Treasury to intervene and influence the value of the dollar against another currency, but in recent years, this has occurred vary rarely. An intervention is occasionally considered necessary to stabilize uncertain markets abroad. The Fed and the Treasury generally coordinate their efforts with the central bank whose currency is being affected.

The New York Federal Reserve Bank performs a variety of financial services for foreign central banks and international institutions. It maintains accounts, invests funds, acts as agent in the foreign exchange market, and provides vault facilities for gold. The gold vault under the New York Federal Reserve Bank holds the largest amount of monetary gold in the world.

The Federal Reserve participates in many different international economic forums, organizations, and conferences. The Bank for International Settlements (BIS) in Basel, Switzerland, is an organization made up of the world's central banks. It serves, in effect, as a central bank for central banks and works to promote monetary and financial stability. The Federal Reserve chairman and the president of the New York Federal Reserve represent the Fed in the BIS. Federal Reserve officials also participate in the International Monetary Fund (IMF) and the World Bank.

ARGENTINA'S CRISIS

The U.S. dollar is the currency most used in international transactions. The U.S. economy is the largest in the world. As a result, American economic developments and monetary policy can have a significant effect on economies worldwide.

Thousands of Argentines wait outside a bank for their monthly pension payments in 2002. The government closed banks across the country to prevent bank runs.

The case of Argentina demonstrates the complexities and hazards of managing monetary policy on an international stage. In the early 1990s, Argentina's government took drastic measures to stabilize the country's volatile economic situation. One part of the solution was to fix the rate of the peso—Argentina's currency—to the value of the U.S. dollar. This would stabilize the peso and prevent inflation.

But this policy came at the cost of monetary policy independence. With the peso pegged to the dollar, Argentina could not influence its own money supply. Argentina's monetary policy was essentially linked to U.S. monetary policy, which was not necessarily in the best interest of the Argentine economy. During the late 1990s, the value of the dollar increased. Meanwhile, Argentina's government failed to enact fiscal and labor reforms that would have further bolstered the economy, and the nation slipped into a recession. International pressures worsened its economic situation. Because the peso was tied to the dollar, Argentina could not use monetary tools to counter the downturn.

The situation reached a crisis in 2000 and 2001. Outraged by soaring rates of poverty, inflation, and unemployment, Argentines rose up in protest, sometimes violently. Bank runs further undermined the economy. Argentina then defaulted on its foreign debt in 2001—the biggest such default in history.

Soon afterward, Argentina's president unpegged the peso from the dollar. The nation's economy began to grow, but it took seven years to reach pre-default levels. In 2010, agencies raised Argentina's credit ratings slightly, improving its prospects within the international financial system.

Japan's "Lost Decade"

After the global financial crisis of 2007–2010 took hold, econ-omists looked to Japan as an example of a nation that had experienced a similar situation nearly twenty years earlier. Unfortunately for Japan, though, most experts viewed its mon-etary policy as an example of what not to do when combating a recession.

During the 1970s and 1980s, Japan's economy flourished. In 1989, however, the markets for stocks and real estate quickly collapsed. The government was slow to intervene—in 1992, the interest rate still stood at almost 4 percent and was not lowered. A 4 percent interest rate is too high to support efforts to com-bat a recession. The economy entered a recession plagued by deflation. For years, banks carrying bad loans hid their shaky condition from both the government and the public. The reces-sion stretched out so long that the 1990s became known as Japan's "lost decade."

The U.S. Federal Reserve gleaned some valuable lessons from Japan's situation, which served it and the nation well dur-ing the Great Recession: take aggressive action in a crisis, slash the interest rates, and don't be afraid to pursue unconventional measures if necessary.

Economic Unity in the Eurozone

In 1999, Europe mounted a grand scheme of shared currency. Most of the countries on the continent joined to create a political entity called the European Union (EU). Within the EU, most member nations adopted a common currency, the euro. No longer did European individuals and businesses have to change currency for financial transactions across national borders within Europe. This made it much easier to do business in the eurozone—the nations that use the euro.

The euro linked the member nations together economically. But this union came at the cost of each nation's autonomy over its own economic policy. EU member nations now fall under the authority of the European Central Bank. Like the Federal Reserve, the European Central Bank aims primarily for economic price stability. The monetary policy intended to create overall economic soundness throughout the EU, however, does not always address the specific and particular needs of its member nations.

This became clear in the aftermath of the Great Recession. The member nations of the eurozone entered the EU with different economic liabilities and fiscal policies. For a few countries, this brought problems. Greece's bonds, for example, had long been considered a somewhat risky investment. When Greece adopted the euro, however, investors bought up Greek bonds and enabled the Greek government to go deep into debt. Similarly, countries such as Spain and Ireland were able to borrow more money than they were previously able to before becoming eurozone members. With easier credit, both nations saw the emergence of a housing boom.

The economic downturn hit these debt-ridden countries harder than other eurozone members. Unemployment soared

Riot police clash with protesters during a demonstration in Greece against harsh austerity measures put in place by the government as a condition for a European Union bailout package.

and incomes dropped. If these distressed countries still controlled their own currencies, they could use monetary tools to drop the interest rate and increase the money supply. They could allow the value of their currency to drop against other currencies. Now, however, they were constrained from doing so by the euro.

In 2010, Greece accepted an emergency loan from the EU and IMF on the condition that it put austerity measures into place. The main imperative was to drastically reduce government spending. Ireland also received a bailout in exchange for austerity measures and slashed public spending. Some economists, however, warned that requiring severe budget-cutting measures in these countries could hamper an economic recovery for all the nations experiencing recession worldwide.

CHAPTER SIX

LOOKING TO THE FUTURE

E very economic crisis generally requires decisive action
from the Federal Reserve. Subsequently, the Fed generally
receives harsh criticism from all sides for its course of action.
The aftermath of the Great Recession has been no exception. The
ultraconservative Texas Representative Ron Paul, for example,
published a book in 2009 entitled *End the Fed*. Most criticism
has been slightly more balanced, realistic, and nuanced.

Some critics objected to the huge amounts of money pledged
by the Fed during the severe economic crisis of 2007–2010.
Others believe that the Fed should have taken even more dra-
matic action to prop up and stimulate the economy, even if
that meant going deeper into debt. Many criticized the Fed for
allowing interest rates to remain overly low during the early
2000s, setting the stage for the mortgage and housing crisis
that sparked the wider recession. Others blasted the entire
monetary policy of Greenspan's tenure. There was public fury
all around regarding the bank bailouts. Why should taxpayers
bail out firms that made extremely foolhardy and irresponsible

Ben Bernanke chats with his predecessor, Alan Greenspan. In 2011, Bernanke became the first Fed chairman to appear at a press conference, beginning a new policy of holding regular briefings.

decisions and landed the nation—and the world—in such a mess? Wasn't this just rewarding banks for their incompetence? Shouldn't they be punished instead?

One area of agreement among most critics of the Fed was that steps had to be taken to prevent another such financial crisis from ever developing again. In July 2010, Congress passed a financial regulatory reform bill that increased government oversight of the financial system and created a new Consumer Protection Agency.

LIMITATIONS OF THE FED

After the financial crisis began to wane, the Fed came under intense fire for failing to rein in the housing market and contain the ensuing economic meltdown. Some of this criticism was undoubtedly valid. But the unexpected suddenness and severity of the economic downturn also highlights the limitations of the Fed's power.

The Fed bases its policy decisions on the best available statistics on current economic trends, as well as models and forecasts for the future. This allows a potential for error. In a huge and complicated economy, the Fed must rely on mere estimates and projections when actual, up-to-date, hard data is not yet available. The gap between the economic estimates the Fed works from and the economic realities may be large enough to result in Fed policies that do not address actual economic conditions and may therefore be ineffective or ill-advised.

Monetary policy is by no means the only force influencing the economy. The Fed can anticipate some factors, such as fiscal policy measures. Others, such as natural disasters or international shocks, are impossible to predict. Even when the Fed acts on the best possible models and forecasts, it can take from three months to two years for its actions to affect the economy. With such a long lag, it can be difficult for the Fed to fine-tune a policy decision. When the economy is in crisis, however, the Fed cannot afford to suspend action while waiting for results. It must simply operate based upon the best available information it has at its disposal.

Evolving Transparency and Accountability

The Fed has often faced accusations of being secretive concerning its decision making and eventual actions and policies. In years past, the FOMC would offer little explanation for its actions, policies, or how it had arrived at them. Investors and analysts were left guessing about which economic factors had most influenced policy decisions.

Accusations of secrecy persist, but the Fed has gradually grown much more transparent about its dealings and the rationale behind its decisions. Officials had once feared that releasing details of its deliberations would cause volatility and anxiety in the financial markets. The opposite has proved true. More information gives financial institutions greater confidence in their dealings. In the aftermath of the 1987 stock market crash and the 9/11 attacks, clear statements from the Fed helped reduce financial turmoil.

Federal Reserve officials often give testimony to Congress on economic matters. In 1975, the Fed began a practice of giving monetary reports to Congress twice yearly. In 1979, it began releasing economic projections twice a year. In 2007, this increased to four times a year. During Greenspan's tenure, the Fed began announcing changes to the target federal funds rate and issuing a statement on its decision. In 2011, the Fed chairman instituted a plan to hold quarterly news conferences for the first time in the central bank's history.

The Financial Stability Oversight Council, which includes Ben Bernanke (*center left*) and U.S. Treasury secretary Timothy Geithner (*center*), meets to discuss new rules for preventing future financial crises.

The Fed and Financial Regulatory Reform

The 2010 financial regulatory reform bill—the Dodd-Frank Wall Street Reform and Consumer Protection Act—greatly expanded the government's regulation of financial institutions and markets. Its provisions impact a number of government financial agencies, including the Federal Reserve, the U.S. Treasury, the FDIC, and many others. The act's stated goal was "to promote the financial stability of the United States by improving accountability and transparency in the financial system, to end 'too big to fail,' to protect the American taxpayer by ending bailouts, to protect consumers from abusive financial services practices, and for other purposes."

President Barack Obama signs the Dodd-Frank Wall Street Reform and Consumer Protection Act, a piece of legislation that ushered in sweeping new regulations of the financial industry.

The bill gave the Federal Reserve new responsibilities in developing and implementing rules. It also established the Financial Stability Oversight Council, made up of officials from various top financial regulatory bodies, including the Federal Reserve. The council's purpose is to monitor the activities of big banks and other financial institutions for possible risks to financial stability.

One of the major components of the bill was the creation of a new Bureau of Consumer Financial Protection, an independent bureau within the Federal Reserve. During the housing boom, many borrowers did not recognize the true cost of their mortgages. Fees and rate increases were hidden in the misleading fine print of the contracts. The bureau was established to bring new transparency for consumers making financial decisions, whether in taking out a mortgage or signing up for a credit card. It will require that financial companies give consumers clear and complete information on the costs and features of financial products and services.

GLOSSARY

business cycle Alternating periods of growth and contraction in the economy.

central bank An institution or agency, either associated with the government or independent, that is responsible for exercising control of a nation's monetary and financial systems.

consumer A person or organization that purchases and uses economic goods, especially for personal instead of commercial use.

credit An arrangement to use or possess goods or services on condition of later payment.

currency Something that is used as a medium of exchange; money.

debt Something that is owed or that one is bound to pay to or perform for another.

deflation A sustained drop in general price levels of goods and services.

deposit To place for safekeeping, especially as money in a bank account.

depression A prolonged economic downturn (or trough in the business cycle) marked by high unemployment levels, decreased availability of credit, low investment rates, bankruptcies, bank failures, and deflation.

fiscal policy The use of government spending and taxing powers to influence economic activity.

gross domestic product (GDP) The value of all the goods and services produced in a nation during a period of time, usually a year.

inflation An increase in general price levels of goods and services.

interest A sum paid or charged for the use of money or for borrowing money, often expressed as a percentage of money borrowed and to be paid back within a given time.

investment Money committed in order to earn a future financial return.

money supply Money in the economy that can be exchanged for goods and services.

mortgage A pledge of property, such as a house, as security for a loan to be repaid under specific terms.

recession An economic downturn, usually defined as six months or more of declining GDP.

recovery The upward phase of the business cycle in which economic conditions improve.

stock Ownership shares of a company or corporation.

FOR MORE INFORMATION

Bank of Canada
234 Wellington Street
Ottawa, ON K1A 0G9
Canada
(800) 303-1282
Web site: http://www.bankofcanada.ca
The central bank of Canada, the Canadian counterpart to the
    U.S. Federal Reserve.

Board of Governors of the Federal Reserve System
20th Street and Constitution Avenue NW
Washington, DC 20551
Web site: http://www.federalreserve.gov
The Board of Governors of the Federal Reserve, which is the
    central bank of the United States.

Department of Finance Canada
140 O'Connor Street
Ottawa, ON K1A 0G5
Canada
(613) 992-1573
Web site: http://www.fin.gc.ca
This is the department that oversees the Canadian
    government's budget and spending.

Federal Deposit Insurance Corporation (FDIC)
Public Information Center
3501 North Fairfax Drive
Arlington, VA 22226
(877) 275-3342
Web site: http://www.fdic.gov
The FDIC is the government agency that insures bank deposits.

Federal Reserve Bank of New York
33 Liberty Street
New York, NY 10045
(212) 720-5000
Web site: http://www.newyorkfed.org
This is the largest bank of the Federal Reserve System.

National Economists Club
P.O. Box 19281
Washington, DC 20036
(703) 493-8824
Web site: http://www.national-economists.org
The National Economists Club is a nonprofit, nonpartisan
    organization whose goal is to encourage and sponsor
    discussion and an exchange of ideas on economic trends
    and issues that are relevant to public policy.

U.S. Department of the Treasury
1500 Pennsylvania Avenue NW
Washington, DC 20220
(202) 622-2000
Web site: http://www.treas.gov

The Department of the Treasury's mission is to maintain a strong economy and create economic and job opportunities by promoting the conditions that enable economic growth and stability at home and abroad, strengthening national security by combating threats and protecting the integrity of the financial system, and managing the U.S. government's finances and resources effectively.

WEB SITES

Due to the changing nature of Internet links, Rosen Publishing has developed an online list of Web sites related to the subject of this book. This site is updated regularly. Please use this link to access the list:

http://www.rosenlinks.com/rwe/fed

FOR FURTHER READING

Acton, Johnny, and David Goldblatt. *Economy*. New York, NY: DK, 2010.

Clifford, Tim. *Our Economy in Action*. Vero Beach, FL: Rourke Publishing, 2009.

Connolly, Sean. *The Stock Market*. Mankato, MN: Amicus, 2011.

Craats, Rennay. *Economy: USA Past Present Future*. New York, NY: Weigl Publishers, 2009.

Gilman, Laura Anne. *Economics*. Minneapolis, MN: Lerner Publications, 2006.

Hall, Alvin. *Show Me the Money: How to Make Cents of Economics*. New York, NY: DK, 2008.

Hynson, Colin. *The Credit Crunch* (The World Today). North Mankato, MN: Sea to Sea Publications, 2010.

Landau, Elaine. *The Great Depression*. New York, NY: Children's Press, 2006.

Merino, Noel. *The World Economy* (Current Controversies). San Diego, CA: Greenhaven Press, 2010.

Miller, Debra A. *The U.S. Economy* (Current Controversies). San Diego, CA: Greenhaven Press, 2010.

Riggs, Thomas, ed. *Everyday Finance: Economics, Personal Money Management, and Entrepreneurship*. Detroit, MI: Gale Group, 2008.

Thomas, Lloyd B. *The Financial Crisis and Federal Reserve Policy*. New York, NY: Palgrave Macmillan, 2011.

BIBLIOGRAPHY

Axilrod, Stephen H. *Inside the Fed: Monetary Policy and Its Management, Martin Through Greenspan to Bernanke.* Cambridge, MA: The MIT Press, 2009.

Bernanke, Ben S. "Federal Reserve's Exit Strategy." Testimony before the Committee on Financial Services, U.S. House of Representatives, Washington, DC, February 10, 2010. Retrieved March 2011 (http://www.federalreserve.gov/newsevents/testimony/bernanke20100210a.htm).

Bernanke, Ben S. *"Money, Gold, and the Great Depression."* Remarks at the H. Parker Willis Lecture in Economic Policy, Washington and Lee University, Lexington, VA, March 2, 2004. Retrieved March 2011 (http://www.federalreserve.gov/boarddocs/speeches/2004/200403022/default.htm).

Board of Governors of the Federal Reserve System. "Credit and Liquidity Programs and the Balance Sheet." May 11, 2010. Retrieved March 2011 (http://www.federalreserve.gov/monetarypolicy/bst.htm).

Board of Governors of the Federal Reserve System. *The Federal Reserve System: Purposes and Functions.* 9th ed. Washington, DC: Board of Governors of the Federal Reserve System, 2005.

Board of Governors of the Federal Reserve System. "The Structure of the Federal Reserve System." June 8, 2003. Retrieved March 2011 (http://www.federalreserve.gov/pubs/frseries/frseri.htm).

Carlson, John, et al. "Credit Easing: A Policy for a Time of Financial Crisis." Federal Reserve Bank of Cleveland, February 11, 2009. Retrieved March 2011 (http://www.clevelandfed.org/research/trends/2009/0209/02monpol.cfm).

Epping, Randy Charles. *The 21st Century Economy: A Beginner's Guide*. New York, NY: Vintage Books, 2009.

Federal Reserve Bank of Kansas City. *The Balance of Power: The Fight for an Independent Central Bank, 1790–Present*. Kansas City, MO: The Public Affairs Department of the Federal Reserve Bank of Kansas City, 2009.

Federal Reserve Bank of New York. "Fedpoints." Retrieved March 2011 (http://www.newyorkfed.org/aboutthefed/fedpoints.html).

Federal Reserve Bank of New York. "What We Do." March 2010. Retrieved March 2011 (http://www.newyorkfed.org/aboutthefed/whatwedo.html).

Federal Reserve Bank of Pennsylvania. "A Day in the Life of the FOMC: An Inside Look at the Federal Reserve's Monetary Policymaking Body." 2008. Retrieved March 2011 (http://www.philadelphiafed.org/education/teachers/resources/day-in-life-of-fomc/#09).

Federal Reserve Bank of Richmond. *The Federal Reserve Today*. 16th ed. Richmond, VA: Federal Reserve Bank of Richmond, 2009.

Federal Reserve Bank of San Francisco. *The Federal Reserve System in Brief*. San Francisco, CA: Federal Reserve Bank of San Francisco, 2006.

Federal Reserve Bank of San Francisco. *U.S. Monetary Policy: An Introduction*. San Francisco, CA: Federal Reserve Bank of San Francisco, 2004.

"Federal Reserve System." *New York Times*, October 3, 2010. Retrieved March 2011 (http://topics.nytimes.com/top/reference/timestopics/organizations/f/federal_reserve_system/index.html?inline=nyt-org).

Ferguson, Roger W., Jr. "September 11, the Federal Reserve, and the Financial System." Remarks at Vanderbilt University, Nashville, TN, February 5, 2003. Retrieved March 2011 (http://www.federalreserve.gov/boarddocs/speeches/2003/20030205/default.htm).

Gordon, John Steele. *An Empire of Wealth: The Epic History of American Economic Power*. New York, NY: HarperCollins, 2004.

Gorman, Tom. *The Complete Idiot's Guide to the Great Recession*. New York, NY: Penguin, 2010.

Gross, Daniel. *Dumb Money: How Our Greatest Financial Minds Bankrupted the Nation*. New York, NY: Free Press, 2009.

Hafer, R. W. *The Federal Reserve System: An Encyclopedia*. Westport, CT: Greenwood Press, 2005.

Johnson, Roger T. *Historical Beginnings . . . The Federal Reserve*. Boston, MA: Federal Reserve Bank of Boston, 1999.

Martin, Preston, and Lita Epstein. *The Complete Idiot's Guide to the Federal Reserve*. Indianapolis, IN: Alpha Books, 2003.

Nechio, Fernanda. "The Greek Crisis: Argentina Revisited?" Federal Reserve Bank of San Francisco Economic Letter, November 1, 2010. Retrieved March 2011 (http://www.frbsf.org/publications/economics/letter/2010/el2010-33.html).

OpenCongress.org. "Text of H.R.4173 – Dodd-Frank Wall Street Reform and Consumer Protection Act." Retrieved March 2011(http://www.opencongress.org/bill/111-h4173/text).

Tucker, Irvin. *Economics for Today*. 3rd ed. Mason, OH: Thomson/South-Western, 2003.

Wells, Donald R. *The Federal Reserve System: A History*. Jefferson, NC: McFarland & Company, 2004.

Wessel, David. *In Fed We Trust: Ben Bernanke's War on the Great Panic*. New York, NY: Crown Business, 2009.

INDEX

About the Author

Corona Brezina is a writer who often writes on economic subjects. She has previously written books on stimulus plans, deflation, recession, imports and exports, commodities and futures trading, and the GDP and GNP. She lives in Chicago.

Photo Credits

Cover (banner), p. 1 © www.istockphoto.com/Lilli Day; cover (bank), pp. 16–17, 24–25, 34–35, 50–51, 61, 64 Bloomberg via Getty Images; pp. 6, 28–29 Britt Leckman, Federal Reserve Photo; pp. 8, 19, 32, 45, 52, 60 ghosted photo by Mario Tama/Getty Images; p. 9 Chip Somodevilla/Getty Images; p. 11 http://en.wikipedia.org/wiki/File:Erie_and_Kalamazoo_Banknote_1853.jpg; p. 14 Courtesy of the Woodrow Wilson Presidential Library, Staunton, Virginia; p. 20 Ryan McVay/Photodisc/Thinkstock; p.23 http://en.wikipedia.org/wiki/File:Federal_Reserve_Districts_Map.svg; p. 36 Mark Ralston/AFP/Getty Images; pp. 38–39 Rolls Press/Popperfoto/Getty Images; p. 42 © AP Images; p. 47 Kevork Djansezian/Getty Images; p.53 © Stock Connection/SuperStock; p.55 © Reuters/Enrique Marcarian/Landov; p. 59 Aris Messinis/AFP/Getty Images; p. 65 AFP/Getty Images; cover and interior graphic elements: © www.istockphoto.com/Andrey Prokhorov (front cover), © www.istockphoto.com/Dean Turner (back cover and interior pages), © www.istockphoto.com/articular (p. 31); ©www.istockphoto.com/DarjaTokranova(p.44);©www.istockphoto.com/studiovision (pp. 67, 69, 72, 73, 77); © www.istockphoto.com/Chen Fu Soh (multiple interior pages).

Designer: Nicole Russo; Photo Researcher: Amy Feinberg